LIAR

Exposing Myths
In Spiritual Warfare

MARK CASTO

Foreword by Damon Thompson

Dedication

To my Father, Damon Thompson, for
forging a way out of the system so that a
wanderer like me could find home.

Far more problematic than a principality is our wandering eyes from Face-to-Face communion with Yahweh. In this book, Mark Casto has set his heart to adjust those wandering eyes from being enamored with darkness and to get our devotional gaze singly fixed on Jesus and the victory He's provided. That's my kind of book! Well written and processed out of a place of peace with a hope for a more excellent path. I feel this book is saying with Christ, *"Do not rejoice that the spirits are subject to you, but rejoice that your names are written in heaven."*

MATT PETTRY

This work is more than words on a page. It's the invitation to a journey. A journey to a renewed way of thinking, an unshakeable confidence of heart, and a fresh revelation of the supremacy of Jesus. Like classics of faith that have fueled generations before us, each page drips with the grace for reformation and the call of Jesus to come closer and see Him in all of His glorious fullness. I have personally seen the fruit of this message in the life of it's author. It is undeniable and lasting. If that fruit is any indication of what you will experience as a result of reading this work, then I would get started today! Enjoy the journey!

BRYN A. WADDELL

FOREWORD

We have been distracted by an inappropriate obsession with a defeated foe. This revelation has transformed our personal lives as well as our community of burning ones here in The Carolinas. Mark Casto has inherited an extraordinary measure of grace to receive and release this revelation to the world by way of this book that Holy Spirit has entrusted to him.

Many have written on the subject of spiritual warfare over the years but this book is unique because it is not a manual on how to more effectively fight the kingdom of darkness, but rather permission to engage the superior dimension of the Kingdom of Light. I believe you and I could win no greater battle in this life than to inherit victory in the area of personal devotion. We long for a grace that permits the proximity we were predesigned for.

The words you are about to read are intended to become an invaluable resource in the reinforcement of the flame of personal longing. If you truly burn for the uncommon lifestyle of proximity and devotion you were created for, then this revelation will bring you into a measure of truth that will assist in the adjusting of your focus to the one thing lifestyle. This is not casual reading material and it is not more fluffy rhetoric for those that want to play it safe. This is an invitation into a degree of focus on the single priority that is Jesus Himself. If you go forward into this glorious revelation do not be surprised when inferior points of focus begin to fade into the periphery.

It has been such a joy to see this revelation come alive in both Mark and Destani and I am full of hope for so many that will experience an unprecedented degree of focus and pursuit by way of this book.

Go For It,
Damon Thompson

TABLE OF

CONTENTS

PREFACE

I am no stranger to fear. Waking up in sweats and jaws sore from clenching my teeth at night. Anxiety attacks were a frequent visitor to my world. Is this my cross? Are these attacks upon my life due to the calling of God? According to what I was taught this was evidence of the call of God and the proving grounds of a good soldier of Jesus Christ.

Although I was taught to quote *"God does not give the spirit of fear, but of power, love, and a sound mind,"* apparently the finished work was not very finished. My gospel was fragile, my performance determined my acceptance, and whatever trial I faced was either warfare or a foothold I had given the enemy in compromise. I believed a lie.

Raised a Pentecostal, when demons were cast out in our corporate settings, everyone had to plead the blood and take the kids out of the room because evil spirits were looking for new homes. We quoted, *"Whom the Son sets free is free indeed,"* yet we were taught to look over our shoulder because the devil was a roaring lion seeking whom he may devour.

The Saints were always on the defensive. I understood our role to be overcomers because every Christian I knew in my world was in a battle. We never really had testimony services because they were times for testi-moaning. One woman in our little West Virginia church confessed the devil had been on her back all week. As I grew older, I began to wonder with Satan not being omnipresent, why the devil would want to target her, unless she was the Antichrist specifically?

There is no doubt we believed in the finished work of Christ as it related to salvation, but for whatever reason, we could not rest in it. We were always subject to attacks, using an Old Testament example like Job to justify all the demonic activity in our lives. I had accepted this belief system at an early age, and it was reinforced for many years by the men I admired behind the pulpit.

I was the byproduct of poor Pentecostal theology. I was thankful to be raised around the move of God, seeing miracles before my eyes, but there were cracks in the Pentecostal foundation. Refusing to stay a victim I went on a search for the victory that was not possible until I was willing to walk away from all I knew to embrace the mystery of intimacy with Jesus.

Writing this book was something I could not shake, as victory began to grow in my soul, I wanted to share some of the truths that had set me free. At the date of this writing, I am three years free from anxiety attacks and growing in grace instead. I fully believe that the cycle of fear that has plagued my life is over because of the revelation of the finished work and Yahweh's devotion to me.

It's hard now for me to imagine a bride harassed in front of her Bridegroom.

> ## Victory has become personal, no longer a thought left for eternity, but an invitation for the here and now.

I did not feel it necessary to write another book *"laying again"* the foundation of Spiritual Warfare. We can all agree that it is Biblical; however, I want to expose the myths that keep believers in limbo.

I never intended for this book to become a lengthy theological discourse, but an invitation out of war into the lifestyle of devotion to Jesus. This book is not for the world, but for those who have yet to find rest in the good news of Jesus! If we are to see the church in maturity, it will require works of reformation in areas like Spiritual Warfare. I have made it an aim that Yahweh's people will not be destroyed for lack of knowledge.

In this book, you will find all mentions of the words *"war"* and *"warfare"* to be disconnected from your adversary and directly connected to devotion to Jesus. You will discover that access to Eden has been granted, and for you not to make the mistake of Eve and continue an illegal conversation with a serpent. We need a superior fascination with the knowledge of God and begin developing a theology of victory!

It is my prayer that this book will become the provocation needed to get you out of war and resting in the Finished Work of Christ. I hope you will allow this manuscript to become your invitation into face-to-face communion, hidden in the Shadow of the Almighty, free from the fear of dethroned principalities. You were born to walk in the cool of the day with the Creator of the Universe, not to build a war room for spiritual maps and demonic fascination.

May you join me on this new ancient path that leads to life more abundantly, after all, Jesus promised it. I wrote this in a way where you could read it in one sitting; however, I pray that you will not rush through it. I didn't write a book on a collection of facts, even though it is rooted in truth, I want this to be something you experience! So, I hope you wrestle with challenging statements, questioning what you were taught with what you have been confronted with.

I join with the Apostle Paul and pray that *"God, the glorious Father of our Lord Jesus Christ, to give you spiritual wisdom and insight so that you might grow in your knowledge of God. I pray that your hearts will be flooded with light so that you can understand the confident hope he has given to those he called—his holy people who are his rich and glorious inheritance. I also pray that you will understand the incredible greatness of God's power for us who believe him.*

This is the same mighty power that raised Christ from the dead and seated him in the place of honor at God's right hand in the heavenly realms. Now he is far above any ruler or authority or power or leader or anything else—not only in this world but also in the world to come." (Ephesians 1:17-21, NLT)

- Mark Casto, 2018

CHAPTER 1

LIAR

I n the face of religious protest and being banished from Wittenburg, a new sound was heard in the churches of Saxony. From the mouths of martyrs at their death and poor Protestants being forced from their homes, a new song rang out from their lips. It became the national hymn of Protestant Germany, also known as the *"Marseillaise of the Reformation."* We now know it as *"A Mighty Fortress Is Our God."*

Written by the great reformer, Martin Luther, and based on Psalm 46, this hymn is a celebration of the power of God over all spiritual forces and our hope in the finished work of Christ. Tim Challies' said, *"The hymn became closely associated with Luther himself, as it embodied in its words and melody so much of the character of its author-bold, confident, defiant in the face of opposition."* [1]

"The prince of darkness grim,
We tremble not for him;
His rage we can endure,
For lo! His doom is sure.
One little word shall fell him."

It was this third verse that made Luther sing victoriously. But what about that particular verse struck a chord in his heart? In a writing called *"Against Hanswurst,"* Luther writes about himself in the third person,

"For all such books written against me, even if there were as many as thousands of them written every day and every hour, are very easily refuted with the single word, 'Devil, you lie.'

Just as that haughty beggar Dr. Luther sings so proudly and boldly in those words of his hymn, *"One little word shall fell him."*

I don't want to take away from what Luther said, but I think it's easy to conclude that this one word which causes all the plans of Satan to fail is LIAR! Jesus called Satan a *"liar, and the father of lies"* (John 8:44). So would it be a far stretch to say that most of what we hear today in modern-day Spiritual Warfare teaching is the declaration of Satan's own boasting?

Today Satan and his demonic forces are spoken of like they are omnipresent, omniscient, and equal to the Kingdom of God. We paint Warfare like the force in Star Wars, and if we muster up enough strength Light will prevail over darkness. We have made these fallen angels appear to be more than they are in light of the New Covenant and finished work of Christ.

Using the term *"dragon"* several times throughout the book of Revelation, John the Beloved gives us a clue into the deceptive nature of Satan. Interestingly enough, Strong's Definitions Legend writes about the original language, *"drákōn," "(to look); a fabulous kind of serpent (perhaps as supposed to fascinate):-dragon."* Thayer's Greek Lexicon says this is a *"figurative description of the devil."*

I believe John was trying to tell us that this being works to captivate and draw our attention to himself, convincing us that he is more than a serpent. Maybe this describes this generations fascination with studying the kingdom of darkness. Like a serpent, Satan deprives his prey of the ability to resist or escape by the power of a look or gaze. We have become so mesmerized by a serpent's attention to us that we made him into a dragon by our focus, not knowing that our call is to resist not study.

With all of this in mind, I have questions that need to be answered.

If the purpose of Christ's work in the earth was to restore man back to the Garden of God then why are we calling believers to engage the battlefield of the cosmos?

If we are being restored to this Garden-life shouldn't attention and conversation with this sly serpent be avoided as we enjoy walking with Yahweh in the cool of the day?

If Christ disarmed principalities according to the Apostle Paul, then how have they become armed again?

Who painted the picture of Yahweh with a concerned look on His sweaty brow overlooking strategic-level warfare maps trying to configure ways for Divine intervention?

If Satan has no power to create anything then how are we dealing with new hordes of spirits today?

If we are called to be the Light of the world then why have many chosen to give the Kingdom of darkness a spotlight?

These questions are essential if a generation is to see Yahweh and personal identity properly.

 ## A victorious life begins with right thinking about God.

It seems to me we have fallen for the fascination of the Father of Lies. He has stolen the gaze of many today. I have personally witnessed prayer meetings that received more energy addressing evil spirits than the worship of the worthy Lamb! This all changes with one word: ***Liar.***

Spiritual Warfare has become another method to excuse the life of devotion. We have traded *"walking in the cool of the day"* for *"boots on the ground,"* wearing demonic attacks as a badge of honor instead of glowing from face-to-face encounters. So many now look at the Holy Spirit as our commander-in-chief instead of our Comforter and Friend. I'm not sure how five references to *"war"* and *"warfare"* in the New Testament has justified such a militant approach to life within the Kingdom, but the times are changing.

A new breed of believers is being raised in the secret place of devotion. With wide-eyed wonder, they are being captivated by the gaze of God, encountering theology instead of merely studying it. They have moved from the head to the heart, realizing that with restored fellowship to God the study of the demonic seems like such an inferior pursuit. We are beginning to explore Eden and this time we refuse to continue an illegal conversation with a defeated serpent.

CHAPTER 2

LIKE A TEACHABLE CHILD

Radical change is happening. There is no doubt that a new reformation has begun in the body of Christ. New things are being declared and encountered, blueprints are emerging, and new wineskins are being formed. What is being brought forth is not new to the church just new to this generation. God is returning us back to original intent; this is the essence of reformation.

In February of 2016, I had a vision. I saw three men, all recognized by many as Apostles in the church today; sitting on a platform. Above their heads were blue portals which I knew were open heavens and lightning strikes were producing something in their hands. As it began to unfold, I saw that these lightning strikes producing blueprints for the church.

I knew radical changes were to be announced to the remnant. So I asked the Lord, *"How do I stay in step with what you are doing?"* And His response to me was crystal clear. *"It looks like children sitting at my feet."* Since that word came, I have been meditating and writing from this whisper, and I want to begin preparing those who will listen for the radical shift that is happening. I do not know what it all looks like; I just want to share my part. I see many voices from the triumphant remnant that will come forward in the days to come sharing more pieces of the puzzle and how to posture ourselves to receive the new thing the Lord is doing.

In Mark 10:13-16, we see a beautiful picture of what I believe is a key for the days ahead.

"The parents kept bringing their little children to Jesus so that He would lay His hands on them and bless them. But the disciples kept rebuking and scolding the people for doing it. When Jesus saw what was happening, He became indignant with His disciples and said to them, 'Let all the children come to me and never hinder them! Don't you know that God's kingdom realm exists for such as these? Listen to the truth I speak: Whoever does not open their arms to receive God's kingdom like a teachable child will never enter it.' Then he embraced each child, and laying his hands on them, he lovingly blessed each one." (Mark 10:13-16, TPT)

We must become like a teachable child.

We cannot allow religious notions from previous systems and seasons to be the lens of interpretation for what the Holy Spirit is showing us by revelation today.

I am not saying the Bible is not our primary source of guidance, what I am warning is that you don't allow a religious, traditional, or even a denominational notion to keep you from what the Holy Spirit is revealing this day.

The religious spirit will try to exalt man's traditions to the same authority of God's word. It is from this exaltation of tradition that we become hardened to change and fight against the truth. The same spirit of religion that has fought against Elijah, Jeremiah, John the Baptist, Jesus, and Paul still exists today, and we must be prepared to stand our ground.

In the 1500's, Martin Luther was considered a troubled soul, an apostate, author of the Great Apostasy, and corrupter of the church. We now call him the great Reformer. In the 1700's, George Whitfield was shunned by most churches and was forced to preach in fields because he didn't fit the common church traditions. These two men are now considered heroes in church history. How many times have we forced the truth out of the church because we refuse to change?

We cannot be know-it-alls. We must be willing to embrace mystery with child-like wonder and simple trust that Abba Father is leading us. If we ask for bread, will He give us a stone? We also cannot act like what God is saying is not for us. The book of Revelation tells us that John was caught up in the Spirit on the Lord's Day and heard a voice call from behind. I believe it is possible to walk closely with the Lord and still be turned the wrong way. This keeps us humble, never reaching a place of stagnation in the journey and feel we don't have to listen for a new word of direction.

If we are honest, most of what we call maturity in the church today is passionless intellect posing as an intimate pursuit. Jesus spoke of the religious when He said, *"You search the scriptures because you think they give you eternal life. But the scriptures point to me."* (John 5:39, NLT) If scripture does not lead to an encounter with Jesus you are on the path to becoming the same religious individuals who missed the Messiah when He was standing in front of them.

Don't allow yourself to be found in this company. These are the people Jesus called, hypocrites, evil, adulterous, serpents, generation of vipers, fools, blind guides, and whitewashed tombs full of dead men's bones. The only way to keep out of that company is to repent from all FALSE forms of religious maturity in order to embrace what is upon us.

The people who were hindering the little children in Mark 10 were His disciples.

The greatest enemy we will
face in keeping us out of the
lap of Jesus is those posing as
the religiously mature.

I mean this in no disrespect, but the majority of leaders in the current church system will be the ones who will oppose what the childlike find in the lap of Jesus.

What made the disciples rebuke the children and try to keep them away? It was false requirements established by the religious notion that children were not a worthy sense of time for the Messiah. Surely the Messiah does not have time for such childish behavior. This type of thinking is what has produced many self-righteous members in the church but very few sons who walk in kingdom authority.

Jesus quickly rebukes the actions of His disciples. There is no other place Jesus would have you be than pursuing a seat in His lap. He has no greater desire than to bless His children. But I would be wrong not to mention that when you seek Jesus with a one-thing focus you will begin to see past the fake, phony, and false. People will try to talk you out of the pursuit because it rocks the boat of religion and exposes personal compromise. But you keep moving forward and let Jesus handle his leaders.

Some may ask, *"Why would they keep you away from intimacy with Jesus?"* Well just like the Reformation with Martin Luther, your intimacy with Jesus might expose the fact that what we are doing in the church is not Biblical; it will affect their traditions and practices. For some, it will impact their book sales and ministry following. I wish nothing but goodwill for every son and daughter of Yahweh, but some of these things we are doing in the name of *"ministry"* are based off either agenda, ignorance, or tradition, not the truth.

Just imagine for a moment if Peter and those in Acts would have been critical of every detail they were experiencing in the outpouring of the Holy Spirit? Where was the scripture for fire dancing on their heads? Where was the scripture for speaking in other known languages, diverse tongues? Where was the scripture that permitted their shadows to heal the sick? I'm not saying to throw out discernment, but I am calling you out of being critical of everything that doesn't fit your box.

Jesus said to His disciples in Mark 10:14, TPT *"Let all the children come to Me and never hinder them...Whoever does not open their arms to receive God's kingdom like a teachable child will never enter it."* I am asking every one of you who are reading this book to posture your heart like a teachable child. Come humbly and expect God to reveal new things. It's not new; it's just new to this generation who only know the current religious church system!

A NEW ANCIENT PATH

Since October of 2015, I have been on a personal journey and discovery of the ancient path. Looking to answer the call of *"orthodoxy"* first by exiting the current religious system and by way of the wilderness. Like the desert fathers, I'm beginning to see American Christianity, as they did Rome, nominal and the results less spectacular. I had seen crowds with very little fruit of the New Testament standard. I could no longer be satisfied with the opportunities, money, or ministerial success. I wanted the experience of Thomas who encountered a Jesus who could be touched and handled.

It was early into this journey that Yahweh began revealing to me the amount of fear that the average *"Christian"* walks in on a daily basis by exposing it in my own life. Claiming to live a life that trusts God yet hoping to keep our heads above the waters of demonic onslaughts. Not only do most walk in the usual cultural fears but many are bound by the continual reminder that demonic activity is all around. This is not speculation for me, but very personal as I have dealt with fear, panic, and anxiety most of my life while sitting under leaders who helped reinforce these strongholds by an overemphasis on Spiritual Warfare teaching.

A storm of information daily surrounds us. Breaking news, terror, and disasters operate as the lightning strikes, while the thundering voices of political commentators, conspiracy theorists, and social media *"geniuses"* are continually providing information for us to work through. The storm continues to build because our minds offer the perfect atmosphere for it to thrive.

Neuroscience has provided us with many answers that prove our minds are mostly a stress-reactive machine to keep us alive. We become addicted to the news, conspiracies, and fear because our brains are reactive to the stress. Those who influence this world are well aware that if they feed you fear you will come back for more. It puts us in survival mode because we have to know what's going on.

The proof that we live in a culture of fear is that we have moved beyond fear to anxiety. Fear by definition is a response to a present threat. Anxiety, however, is a response to something anticipated or expected to be a threat in the future. According to the National

Institute of Mental Health, approximately 40 million Americans ages 18-54 is affected by anxiety disorders.[2]

New technology and mass media use terrible events to communicate to you that you are never safe. Criminals, terrorists, and sexual predators are lurking around each corner. Every president that rises to power could be the next antichrist and based upon the last commercial you watched you might have a new disease because fear sells.

Sadly, this culture has crept into the America pulpit. Instead of living as ambassadors of the kingdom, we have used the pulpit to continue this fear-based rhetoric. I can't tell you how many times I've had to endure listening to messages filled with conspiracy theories supported with far stretching scriptural interpretation. Not to mention the fear tactics we have used to get people into our altars.

If the early apostles were living today, do you think they would have held conferences giving detailed information about the Deep State? Would they have written entire books on demonic spirits? I don't think so. The apostles would have preached Jesus, crucified, buried, and resurrected. However, this kind of fear-based messages will continue to be taught and thoughtfully packaged because fear sells.

From this culture of fear emerges a battle plan. It is apparent from scripture that we have an adversary, Satan, who has a demonic hierarchy under his control that is made up of principalities, powers, rulers of darkness, and spiritual wickedness in the heavenly places. The Bible tells us not to be ignorant of Satan's devices and that we are to resist these evil forces. From this understanding people have begun to focus on the realm of darkness, some going even as far as to teach on demonology.

While I believe that there is a spiritual war being waged for the soul of man I think that the culture of fear we live in has been the greatest mold for the new spiritual warfare teachings that have emerged these past thirty years.

> **I believe it's time for a new reformation in the church and the area of spiritual warfare needs a significant number of adjustments if we are to mature as the body of Christ.**

What I want to present to you may be offensive and oppose what you have been taught, but it will be Biblical and sound. We need to quit allowing man's traditions and religious myths that have no root in the Bible to keep us in religious bondage.

Unfortunately, in the area of Spiritual Warfare, we have more myths than fruit. This generation is looking for something real. People aren't looking for an eight-page discourse on the Jezebel spirit; they want an encounter with Jesus that conquers every demonic force in their life. They are not fascinated by our messages; they want to see the fruit from what we claim. If God has the power to set men free, heal the sick, and break the chains of demonic bondage, they want it.

Fear is a significant factor in how we interpret many things. But it is not allowed to interpret what comes from the God of Love, for perfect love casts out all fear. God is currently restoring truth back to His church, and the voices of this new reformation will be love struck brides conquered in devotion, not cold-hearted preachers with titles behind pulpits.

I'm taking a stand in the grace of God. I don't want to spend the rest of my life screaming at demons but rather receiving fresh identity that releases authority over all the powers of the enemy. I choose to stand with the voices of fathers and mothers throughout church history so that my roots go deep into God's original intent for man. I hope to share adequately with you the word the Holy Spirit gave to me, that the Church was going to learn how to war a superior way.

As you look at this new path, realize it is not new at all. Many generations have seen few take it, but this ancient road leads to victory. You do not walk alone, for a friend…the Holy Spirit has been assigned as your guide. Look around; a host has surrounded you in the heavenly dimension cheering you on. This new old path may not be the path most convenient, but it is most excellent. So as we journey together, the Lord as our guide, may we be established in the first announcement of the gospel, *"Peace and goodwill towards all men."*

CHAPTER 4

FICTION BASED ON FACTS

All fiction finds its root in the reality of facts. The prolific author, C.S. Lewis, built an entire world of fiction based upon true spiritual realities. His books have given us incredible revelation of spiritual truths through fictional characters, stories, and his writings have now become movies. However, with that same creativity, we take the risk of creating myth upon myth until reality is lost.

Spiritual warfare finds its roots in Biblical truth. But over the years people have taken verses of the Bible and built myth upon myth until now I believe the reality of these truths have been distorted or even lost. So before you start sending me emails, let's build a foundation that we can all agree upon for us to take this journey together.

In Revelation 12, John was caught up in the Spirit and saw a war that had broken out in heaven between Michael and his angels and the Dragon with his angels. The ancient serpent, that dragon, the devil, the deceiver of the whole world was cast down to the earth. According to 1 Peter 5:8 we know that the devil is on the prowl like a roaring lion seeking someone he MAY devour. His very name means *"adversary," "one who opposes,"* and *"slanderer."*

We know there is a war taking place in the Spirit realm for the soul of man. Satan is our adversary along with his demonic hierarchy in the unseen realm, recorded by Paul in Ephesians 6:12. The vast majority of this world is held in bondage to Satan and is unaware. Jesus said of Satan in John 14:30, that he was the ruler of this world. What does he do as a ruler?

- Blinds the mind of unbelievers (2 Cor. 4:4)
- The Spirit at work in the children of disobedience (Ephesians 2:2)
- He is an accuser of believers in Christ (Rev. 12:10)
- He the tempter of man (Matt. 4:3; 1 Thess. 3:5)
- He is the deceiver of mankind (Gen. 3; Rev. 20:3)

You thought I was ready to make the announcement that I had dismissed the kingdom of darkness? In fact, I do recognize we have an adversary and that there is a war. But I want to submit to you that the path we have been taught to overcome has become very mythical which can help explain why most engaged in warfare around us are not walking in life more abundantly.

The purpose of my writing is to expose the error we have made in recent generations to overemphasize the subject of Spiritual Warfare. Although, this will not be an exhaustive work I hope to uncover a few unbiblical myths so that we might receive new blueprints for victory today. We live in a day where the gospel is fragile, and the work of our adversary is continuously highlighted. We have allowed poor theology to identify us as survivors waiting for the rapture instead of overcomers advancing the Kingdom of God on earth as it is in heaven.

> In the absence of true apostolic preaching of the gospel of the Kingdom, we have allowed our ears to be tickled by those infatuated with "revelation" on the kingdom of darkness.

In our fear, we have latched onto these myths and allowed one aspect of the Great Commission, to cast out devils, to replace the first and greatest commandment. This curiosity with the dark world has opened our minds to grand delusions, beginning with the lie of increased demonic activity in our day.

Many people believe that Satan is unleashing new spirits that we have never faced before as Christians in these *"last days."* Have you read the latest from the peddlers of products? Again, I have so many questions, Does Satan have the power to create? Does the eternal realm operate by a 12 hour period called *"night?"* Can demons be fruitful and multiply?

If the demonic realm was going to multiply why didn't Jesus and the apostles not dedicate more time to this subject? Make the madness stop! Satan fell with a third of the angels of heaven, and that is what he still has today. Which still leaves God's kingdom with two-thirds of the angelic host on our side.

Many would say that it is more evil today than ever before. Has not every generation said that? We no doubt have plenty of opportunities for sin with the increase of technology and access to almost anything in the world by our phone, but is this our darkest hour? We are dealing with the same spirits that existed since the fall of Lucifer and his angels. There have been more evil days. Have you ever read *"Foxe's Book of Martyrs"*?

During the days of the early church, Christians were regularly attacked. Believers were burned to death at the Circus Maximus in Rome. For Nero's birthday or any special holiday, he would request an afternoon for Christian martyrdom in the Coliseum. Capacity crowds would gather to watch wild animals eat Christians alive. Some Christians were even used as human torches to give light for Roman workers during the night. There have been more evil days.

Should we take a look into something more current like the twentieth century? From World War I, World War II, the Holocaust, Stalin's Soviet Union, and Chairman Mao's Communist China, has the world grown worse? Mao's demonic aspirations cost China 35-45 million lives in the Great Leap Famine alone. Hitler was responsible for approximately 11 million deaths in the

Holocaust, and Stalin's systematic killing of people in the Soviet Union destroyed the lives of nearly 60 million human beings.

We have been in the last days for 2,000 years, and every generation gets to see its share of darkness. But we are the church Jesus said the gates of hell could not prevail against. In every evil day, the church has continued to multiply and go from glory to glory. Our focus should not be upon well-intentioned pre-tribulation rapture theorists infatuation with supposed increase demonic activity when we have Isaiah, Joel, and John the Beloved prophesying to us such hope for global transformation.

It's hard to believe we are more than conquerors when you rarely hear messages on *"growing in grace"* but are inundated with messages on *"increased demonic activity."* This is error.

We cannot allow fear mongering ministers to give the demonic realm creative abilities reserved for Yahweh alone.

This false teaching of *"increased"* demonic activity is an indictment upon us as image bearers of Christ.

CHAPTER 5

MISINTERPRETING VERSES

Depending on the translation, the words *"war"* or *"warfare"* are used five times in the New Testament. However, each time they are used it has zero connection to the devil but rather exhortations for us to conquer the flesh and take charge over our minds. Let me explain.

It's what I call the *"Scooby Doo Effect."* Many of you grew up watching this classic cartoon show featuring four teenagers, Shaggy, Fred, Velma, Daphne, and their talking Great Dane *"Scooby-Doo."* Each episode is about solving mysteries that involve supposed supernatural creatures. After several minutes of twists and turns they discover not a supernatural being, but a dysfunctional person wearing a mask.

I am not trying to belittle the reality of warfare, but I have found that many who are always in a fight or confronting another spirit are playing right into the trick of the garden deceiver. The problem is not the devil;

> ## we are masking our dysfunction in the name of spiritual warfare while excusing ourselves from the need to renew our minds.

If we are to take any advice from the *"Scooby-Doo"* show, let's pull the mask of fabricated spiritual warfare off and allow the Holy Spirit to lead us into a renewed mind.

Where do we begin? We start here with the five main verses used in the New Testament to form our understanding of how the words *"war"* and *"warfare"* is to be understood in the life of the believer. Get ready for a surprise; your greatest enemy is about to be revealed.

Our first reference is found in 1 Timothy 1:18 where Paul is encouraging Timothy to hold on to the prophetic words that were spoken over his life. Paul, in essence, encourages Timothy that these words will help him *"war a good warfare."* But what war are we talking about? The battle between Light and Darkness? No, by looking at this verse in context Paul is encouraging Timothy in the fight of faith.

Paul was encouraging his son in the faith to use these words as strength to remain faithful to the call of God upon his life. Could this verse be helpful while facing actual *"spiritual warfare?"* The Liar would have you believe something different, but this verse has zero indication of a connection with the Devil, rather faithfulness to Jesus.

The second reference I want to highlight is found in 2 Timothy 2:3-4. Paul wrote to Timothy, *"You therefore must endure hardship as a good soldier of Jesus Christ. ⁴No one engaged in warfare entangles himself in the affairs of this life, that he may please Him who enlisted him as a soldier."*

Paul is using the example of a soldier to illustrate the way Timothy should act during suffering or hardship. The example is to be single-minded and committed to pleasing the one who called him. This has nothing to do with the devil, but rather that Timothy would remain focused upon Jesus as he goes through the trials of this life. How far have we missed the mark in just one verse?

This may be the primary verse used to solidify our identity as a warrior fighting evil spirits in a cosmic battle. But this verse is not Paul's attempt to focus Timothy on our adversary, but rather to fix his gaze upon the one who has called him, Jesus. This passage alone has become the wind and waves that have sunk many water-walkers.

Do you remember when Jesus called Peter to Himself in the midst of a great storm? Peter was walking on water in the supernatural dominion available to all who answer the call of Christ until he began to look at his circumstances. When Peter took his eyes off of Jesus, he sank. Paul is not teaching young Timothy here about how to war, but how to walk!

If you take this verse as ammunition for demons instead of single-mindedness in devotion to Jesus, then you have taken the bait of the Liar, and you will never please Him who enlisted you. This is the first example of many where people used one verse to call you to war instead of showing you how to walk with Him in the cool of the day.

The Apostle Peter writes our third example in 1 Peter 2:11, which reads, *"Beloved, I beg you as sojourners and pilgrims, abstain from fleshly lusts which war against the soul."*

This verse has no connection with the demonic, but rather the fleshly lusts within the human nature. Can the enemy try to influence our minds and our carnal nature? Yes. But beloved, we give the Liar too much credit. Look at the verses in context, and you will find that you don't need any help doing wrong. In just two verses, the cat is already out of the bag. Your greatest enemy is not the devil it's you.

Example number four enforces the previous verse. James 4:1 says *"Where do wars and fights come from among you? Do they not come from your desires for pleasure that war in your members?"* Another verse about war and the common denominator is the fleshly desires within, not the devil. Do you see it yet? This war is being played out in your flesh and mind.

Our last example is a verse that I learned to quote as a young Pentecostal warring against the release of Dan Brown's 2006 film, *"The Da Vinci Code."* I remember Pastors buying books from zealous Christian authors to sell to the flock because this movie was infused with evil spirits destined to destroy the Faith. I'm not sure of the exact outcome, but somebody made a lot of money.

The verse… *"For though we walk in the flesh, we do not war according to the flesh. ⁴For the weapons of our warfare are not carnal but mighty in God for pulling down strongholds, ⁵casting down arguments and every high thing that exalts itself against the knowledge of God, bringing every thought into captivity to the obedience of Christ,"* (2 Cor. 10:3-5)

This verse speaks of mental strongholds that must be *"pulled down."* Rick Renner comments on this verse in his remarkable book, *"Dressed to Kill"* saying, *"It is true that these bondages and strongholds in the mind may have first attached themselves to us in the past when we were still under Satan's control. However, we must keep these verses in their proper context. In context, these verses are referring to a person making an immovable decision to take charge of his mind and take thoughts of his mind captive."*

In an entitled world where we want everything handed to us, we would instead punt to Providence with our mental bondages than take responsibility for them.

Encounters are essential to the life of the believer; however, they provide the grace through the Spirit of God to dismantle any thought process that exalts itself above two things (1) the knowledge of God and (2) obedience to Christ.

Paul is showing the church in Corinth that these mental bondages are not to be excused by demonic activity, but instead, they have a responsibility through the grace of God to combat these old ways of fleshly thinking through the knowledge of God.

Notice Paul did NOT say that we must understand the seven characteristics of Jezebel, draw out a spiritual map, and repent on behalf of our ancestors, to cast down this stronghold. The weapon that is mighty in God to pull down these strongholds and become obedient to Christ is to make sure we let nothing exalt itself against the KNOWLEDGE OF GOD.

CHAPTER 6

AN ILLEGAL
CONVERSATION

The New Testament examples I have given you in the previous chapter prove that even the verses which contain the mention of warfare are in the context of devotion to Jesus. Paul and Peter both encourage us to be faithful to the call of God, to stay single-minded in order to please the One who called, abstaining from fleshly lusts that war against our soul, and bringing our every thought into captivity to the obedience of Christ through the knowledge of God! Does this sound like today's teaching on Spiritual Warfare?

These five verses should posture our hearts for Adam's original mandate in Eden and provide answers for how we are to subdue the enemy. His commission to Adam and Eve was to *"be fruitful and multiply. Fill the earth and govern it."* (Gen. 1:28, NLT). God never once mentioned that outside of His Garden of Perfection was a Kingdom of Darkness that hated Yahweh and all that He had created.

I believe God desired for Adam to walk with Him and through intimate single-minded fellowship, man through dominion would cover the earth with the glory of the Lord. Through devotion alone, it would produce natural dominion, giving the enemy no place to remain. In essence, our communion would have permanently driven Satan off of the planet.

> # Adam did not live in the reality of an adversary but lived in response to the Presence of Yahweh.

With each step of obedience to the original mandate, the garden's borders would expand, and Satan would lose more territory without Adam's knowledge. Yahweh did not give Adam instructions for warfare, but access to His Presence was all that was necessary. It was when man started having conversations with inferior beings that problems arose in the garden.

Eve's conversation with the serpent led to man's agreement with God's adversary, and this is where spiritual warfare finds it roots concerning the human race. The serpent engaged the mind to make her question the truth that was supposed to govern her spirit. Today we are making that same mistake instead of being ruled by the Spirit of Truth we engage our minds and expand our expertise in the knowledge of good and evil. After the cross, many are still eating from the wrong tree.

> ## Most of what we are being taught today as it relates to spiritual warfare is nothing more than the continuation of an illegal conversation Eve had with the serpent in the garden.

Yahweh in His jealousy is going to judge this overemphasis of spiritual warfare in our day because it is glorifying the Liar and taking away from the walks He longs to have with His beloved in the cool of the day.

Thankfully, 2000 years ago Jesus came to another garden with the sin of Adam and hung it on the tree so that we could be restored back to the original mandate of devotion to Him alone. Jesus gave us access back to the garden of God's pleasure, so why waste your time entertaining conversations with the enemy when you have access to such a high degree of Presence!

This overemphasis on spiritual warfare is an insult to the finished work of Christ, His blood, His grace, and His Precious Holy Spirit. Jesus didn't die on the cross for you to continue a conversation with a serpent. He desires to take a walk with you as He walked with Adam in His garden. I believe I hear the Lord calling, *"Adam, where are you?"* Not because He doesn't know where you are, but it's to see if you know where you are.

Many have taken an intellectual ascent into this fictional approach to Spiritual Warfare and have begun to strut on a fabricated battlefield covering themselves in the fig leaves of their personal effort. While the Spiritual Warfare camp boasts in their sacrifice, works, labor, travel, and toil they fail to realize that reproduction doesn't happen on the battlefield, but rather in the bedchamber.

Paul was concerned for the church of Corinth in this same regard when he said, *"For I am jealous for you with godly jealousy. For I have betrothed you to one husband, that I may present you as a chaste virgin to Christ. ³But I fear, lest somehow, as the serpent deceived Eve by his craftiness, so your minds may be corrupted from the simplicity that is in Christ."* (2 Cor. 11:2-3, NKJV) Paul was convinced that there is an enemy; however, he wanted the focus of the believers to be of *"singleness of mind."*

Paul's concern was for what another translation would call, *"simplicity and purity of devotion."* (2 Cor. 11:3, NASB) Where is the simplicity in Spiritual Warfare? Where is the purity of devotion in the teaching of demonology? Is it in our drawing of maps for strategic-level warfare, identifying principalities over regions, or our drawing attention away from Christ to focus on understanding the characteristics of Korah and Jezebel?

> Our fictional overemphasis on the demonic world and spiritual warfare is robbing us of simple and pure devotion to Jesus.

Yahweh is calling for His sons; Jesus is calling for His bride, to come back to the garden of devotion.

I know what you are thinking. How can you call us off the battlefield and into the bedchamber in such a crucial hour? I would ask those of you who believe we are getting snatched off the planet during the world's most important hour of tribulation the same question. But my confidence comes from the knowledge of who I am communing with. I trust His nature, attributes, and character. I have seen His mighty works and experienced His world.

The Light is exposing the lies and the Liar. I am continuing to learn about the Father, the Son, and His Spirit. I have read of cherubim, seraphim, and Michael. I even meditate on John the Beloved's account in Revelation 20:1-2 that one UNKNOWN angel can bind the dragon for a thousand years. This is the hour of great dominion, and it will not come from the proficiency of our sword, but rather from our unwavering commitment to one thing: the Great Commandment.

"We love Him, because He first loved us." - 1 John 4:19, KJV

CHAPTER 7

A SUPERIOR FASCINATION

I still remember as a little boy when a man introduced a book to my father called, *"Pigs In The Parlor."* Within a few weeks, special deliverance services were being conducted at our church. I watched as this man would start asking questions to those seeking deliverance. Then once a question struck a chord, the process began. He went from talking to the person to a manifested demon. Scriptures were quoted, sometimes physical altercations would occur, then the process usually ended with a trash can full of green goo.

It was all so strange to me. For years I had watched my father minister in the anointing of the Holy Ghost and when demons manifested they were just cast out without any extra fanfare. But it was apparent that things were changing. More personalities began to emerge like Bob Larson who would perform exorcisms, interview Satanists, and would slap the Bible on the demon-possessed foreheads.

Through one book, deliverance ministry was in full effect in our little church. People began experiencing demonic activity in their homes. Strange phenomenon was being reported, and people who were Christians were being convinced they had been demon-possessed without knowing it. Thankfully these people began to pray and realize the truth. The increase everyone was experiencing in the realm of darkness was because darkness had become their focus. Just as quick as that overemphasis came into our church, it went back out.

Many of you may have never experienced this, but some have. This demon-conscious style of ministry has gained momentum the past thirty years, and although it may not be as dramatic as making a public spectacle of demon possession, nevertheless it still has a strong influence in Spirit-filled circles and sermons.

Just read through prophetic websites or Spirit-filled news and you will undoubtedly find the latest attack upon the saints and the names of these demonic spirits. I'm sure by now you have heard countless messages on Jezebel or Leviathan. While demonic spirits are real, I cannot figure out why certain individuals are so fascinated with them when there is a superior fascination available in the life of devotion? If we hope to see the Kingdom of darkness eradicated from the earth, then that work must begin within us first by eliminating any fascination we have with that realm.

Serving in the position of youth pastor for a few years, I felt the need to wade through the murky waters of the culture's impact on the students I lead. Because of my immaturity at that time I thought I was responsible for helping them understand the demonic realm behind the culture they flirt with. I began studying the entertainment and music industries, the personalities being promoted, and the conspiracy theories behind their power. I found everything from the Illuminati to people that had sold their souls to the devil to be the best.

This world of conspiracy and the study of demonic forces can spark curiosity. This dark world of the unknown is very appealing to study because we are seekers at the very core of our nature. But this study is very fascinating to an individual who lacks the devotional experience of knowing the nature of God. I want to caution those of you who are being pulled away by the fascination of demons. Your unholy interest in pursuing a study on darkness may be the doorway to this overemphasis on Spiritual warfare.

During my time of uncovering information about the dark world of the entertainment industry, I began to experience strong attacks and temptations. I don't mean this in a self-righteous way, but I was frustrated that these thoughts were attacking my mind because it was things that I had gained victory over when I gave myself to the Lord. After having a conversation with a father in my life, I got the best advice possible.

"You have given the enemy access to your mind because you have given those spirits your attention and focus."

That's when this verse became a revelation to me. *"But we all, with unveiled faces, beholding as in a mirror the glory of the Lord, are being transformed into the same image from glory to glory, just as by the Spirit of the Lord."* (2 Cor. 3:18, NKJV) This verse gives us the spiritual principle that you become what you behold. This has been proven to me by personal experience and discernment over the years. Nearly every person I know that has done an in-depth study on a demonic spirit will begin to manifest the influence or have to fight that spirit in his or her own life. If you study Jezebel, you will fight her manifestation in you. Because you become what you behold.

The excuse many people make is that we are not to be ignorant of Satan's devices. (2 Cor. 2:11) I agree we are not to be ignorant of Satan's devices; however, that is not permission for us to become experts either. That's like saying that God would have been okay with sharing Eve's focus with the serpent in the garden. Now we have entire movements in the body of Christ who have become experts in Satan's devices but novices in the attributes of God. If we are to come out of this fabrication of darkness, we need a superior fascination: the knowledge of God.

As we learned in chapter 5, the way we pull down strongholds is by casting down any high thing that exalts itself against the knowledge of God. The knowledge of God is the foundation for faith, identity, and victory in this life! One revelation of Yahweh can wipe away the culture of fear, negativity, and conspiracy we have been raised in.

A.W. Tozer said, *"What comes into our minds when we think about God is the most important thing about us."* This becomes an extraordinary place of renewal that must take place in our minds if we hope to be less *"demon conscience"* and step into the Kingdom life of *"righteousness, peace, and joy in the Holy Ghost."* In the book of Daniel 11:32 we receive another key for us when the ancient language of Aramaic bears out this translation: *"They that know their God intimately, will find their reason for existence."*

How can we image forth our Creator correctly if we are ignorant of His nature and attributes? How we see Yahweh determines our faith and expectations in this life and the one to come. This knowledge is not to be read-only, but more importantly, experienced. Our loving God wants to break the power of fear in of our lives and bring us to our closest proximity. There is a higher path of victory, and it's not by understanding the strength of our enemy, but being convinced of the Superiority of the Almighty God!

CHAPTER 8

DEVELOPING
VICTORY THEOLOGY

B efore we dive into more specifics, I want to clearly state that I believe our pathway to victory is the knowledge of God! It is not enough to expose myths; we have to renew our minds and develop victory theology. This understanding of God is rooted in His love as a Father and His immutable goodness. From Abba's love to Jesus' finished work we find ourselves. We begin to inherit proper identification as the beloved sons and daughters of God, and we start to see nothing as impossible!

This idea of victory finds its origin in the Torah. The concept of victory among the Israelites was something that ultimately comes from the Lord. His Presence among them guaranteed the victory. God began revealing Himself as their Defender when the children of Israel left Egypt. After separating them from Pharaoh's army by fire, God Himself twisting their chariot wheels, to drowning them in the Red Sea, Yahweh was making a statement.

In Deuteronomy 20:4, God promised to fight against Israel's enemies, and He would give them the victory. In 2 Chronicles 20:17, the Prophet Jahaziel stood up and declared to the people of Judah that they need not fight, but stand still and see the Lord's salvation. Not to mention Gideon and his three hundred men who caused an entire army to flee and turn on itself with broken pots, torches, and shouts, proving that military superiority was not a prerequisite for victory!

Zechariah, the prophet, revealed God as a warrior who gives the victory. Isaiah went as far as saying that when no human is there to intervene, it would be the Lord's own arm that brings victory. In many Biblical cases, people prepared for battle, but they all understood that victory belongs to the Lord. Isaiah saw a day of victory coming when He prophesied,

"Nevertheless, that time of darkness and despair will not go on forever. The land of Zebulun and Naphtali will be humbled, but there will be a time in the future when Galilee of the Gentiles, which lies along the road that runs between the Jordan and the sea, will be filled with glory. ²The people who walk in darkness will see a great light. For those who live in a land of deep darkness, a light will shine. ³You will enlarge the nation of Israel, and its people will rejoice.

They will rejoice before you as people rejoice at the harvest and like warriors dividing the plunder. ⁴For you will break the yoke of their slavery and lift the heavy burden from their shoulders. You will break the oppressor's rod, just as you did when you destroyed the army of Midian. ⁵The boots of the warrior and the uniforms bloodstained by war will all be burned. They will be fuel for the fire. ⁶For a child is born to us, a son is given to us. The government will rest on his shoulders. And he will be called: Wonderful Counselor, Mighty God, Everlasting Father, Prince of Peace. ⁷His government and its peace will never end. He will rule with fairness and justice from the throne of his ancestor David for all eternity. The passionate commitment of the Lord of Heaven's Armies will make this happen!" (Isaiah 9:1-7)

Can you see it? At the coming of Christ regions in the earth are filled with His glory. Light begins to invade the darkness, people are rejoicing, yokes destroyed, burdens removed from necks, and the boots and uniforms bloodstained by battle are all burned. Why, because a Child has been born. His government and its peace will never end. Isaiah ends the prophecy by saying it is the Lord of Heaven's Armies passionate commitment that will make this possible.

When the announcement of Jesus birth came from the angelic hosts to shepherds abiding in the field, they said, *"Glory to God in the highest realms of heaven! For there is peace and a good hope given to the sons of men."* (Luke 2:14, TPT) There is no announcement of peace unless victory is accomplished. Our assurance of that peace comes through the purpose of His revealing. *"The reason the Son of God was revealed was to undo and destroy the works of the devil."* (1 John 3:8, TPT)

In Matthew 12:28 Jesus announced the end of Satan's Kingdom and that it was time to gather the spoils. Paul informed the church in Colosse that *"Jesus made a public spectacle of all the powers and principalities of darkness, stripping away from them every weapon and all their spiritual authority and powers to accuse us. And by the power of the cross, Jesus led them around as prisoners in a procession of triumph. He was not their prisoner; they were His!"* (Col. 2:15, TPT) Now we by the authority of Christ given unto the church use dethroned principalities as our footstools. This sounds like victory to me!

John the Beloved wrote a single passage that I believe should frame our whole concept of victory. The victory that triumphs over the world is our faith, and there is only one requirement for those who will reign in victory, belief in Jesus as the Son of God. (1 John 5:4-5) I know what you are thinking. It cannot be that simple. But, friend,

we cannot make theology adapt to the multiplicity of our circumstances, we are being called back to simplistic devotion.

Our pure faith in Christ alone makes us overcomers. If we see being an overcomer by faith in Christ alone, then it should change how we even interpret the language of victory that saturates the messages to the seven churches in Revelation. Here are the promises of victory to the overcomer:

- Yahweh grants us access back to the tree of Life in the paradise of God (Rev. 2:7)
- We are not subject to the second death. (2:11)
- We receive hidden manna, a new name (2:17)
- We receive power over the nations, to rule over them (2:26-27)
- Our names are inscribed in the Book of Life (3:5)
- We are made a pillar in the temple of God (3:12)
- We are seated on the Lord's throne with Him (3:21)

However, do not stop with the message of the seven churches. Revelation gives us the ultimate picture of victory when Christ mounts His white horse riding forth to conquer (6:2), and together with Christ, we conquer the kingdom of the beast (17:14). But here is what victory with Christ is all about: *"The conquering ones will inherit these gifts from Me. I will continue to be their God, and they will continue being children for me."* (Rev. 21:7) This theology of victory equips us to know that all victory belongs to the Lord and it is for one purpose, that we may belong to Him.

Victory for Yahweh is not Satan cast into the lake of fire.

Victory for Yahweh is restored fellowship with His sons and daughters.

It means intimacy, being one in the Garden of His pleasure, face-to-face communion, unhindered by the sounds of war.

CHAPTER 9

THE ARMOR OF GOD

When I first started sharing some of the truths in this book people continued to bring up Ephesians 6:10-18 to prove that we are in a war. As you now know, I do not disagree that there is a war. However, I believe it's no longer the previous religious definition of *"warfare,"* it's exercising authority from a place of victory! The continual reminder of this passage along with a vital instruction from my Apostle has led me to take time and focus on the *"Armor of God."*

How many messages have you heard on the whole armor of God? Men and women have spent countless hours researching the physical armor of the Roman soldier in Paul's day. I have witnessed incredible illustrated messages over the years correlating the armor of the Roman soldier and how it relates to our spiritual armor that is given to us. Although these messages are good, we have overemphasized the Roman soldier's equipment just like we have the demonic realm.

There is no doubt that the Holy Spirit highlighted to Paul the Roman soldier's equipment to develop an analogy. However, the reality is that we have the armor of God! For years we have focused on a helmet, breastplate, belt, shield, sword, shoes, and missed the real revelation of salvation, righteousness, truth, faith, the word of God, and peace. With that perspective, we were dressed for battle and never learned to rest in redemption.

Paul gives us a command in Ephesians 6:11, *"Put on the whole armor of God,"* and still in our minds we only think he is talking about warfare. The words *"of God"* in the Greek are *"tou theo,"* and it is written in the genitive case meaning it's not just of God, but from God. God is the source of our armor.

> # If the origin is from God, then intimacy is required to continue enjoying the benefits of what has been provided.

Once again, here is another verse showing that you are protected when you say yes to devotion, not war.

I want to draw your attention to another point that many have overlooked. Although the Roman soldier may have been a piece of inspiration for Paul writing this passage, it was not the source.

Apostle Paul was giving us a complete picture of a prophecy given by Isaiah the Prophet in the 8th century B.C.; Isaiah said of the Messiah, *"For He put on righteousness as a breastplate, And a helmet of salvation on His head;"* (Isaiah 59:17)

The Roman empire began in Rome during the year 753 B.C. and did not conquer and come to power in Israel until 63 B.C. Which lets us know Isaiah was not subject to Roman rule nor had he seen a Roman soldier in his lifetime. This prophecy was a divine revelation of the Messiah and Paul was now stating that because we are one with Christ, we can share in His wardrobe.

Why are we just now discovering these truths? Because, we are in a new reformation, and people are being delivered from an inferior idea of what it means to be armored. The concept of a Roman armor only feels right to a religious spirit who feels the call to war in their works, but a son and daughter are to be fitted with robes and crowns for intimacy and dominion sake.

If we stop at Ephesians 6, we only have one perspective of the armor. We must include 2 Corinthians 6:7, *"the armor of righteousness."* Also, in Romans 13:12 Paul refers to it as *"the armor of light."* Put them all together, and it speaks of the armor as *"of God," "of righteousness,"* which is also *"of light."* All three references to armor in the New Testament speak of devotion, the finished work of Christ, and carries about it the element of light.

Now that we have established the source of the armor of God, should we continue to draw from the inferior analogy of the Roman guard? Don't get me wrong; it helped me get to where I am today. But we must press on to know Him more fully. Are you willing to settle for a helmet when you have been promised a crown? Would you stop with armor when you have been given the command to put on Christ Himself?

Let's begin with the helmet of salvation. This piece of armor is not the helmet of a Roman soldier; it is salvation. The reality of salvation is what protects your mind and silences the voice of the accuser. I thank God for this understanding of salvation, but I don't plan to stay in the infantry. The root word of *"infantry"* is *"infant."* Those in the infantry were the foot soldiers who were considered *"low"* in rank due to their inexperience.

The Lord wants to move you from a helmet to a crown. There are five crowns you can receive as a believer, but the one I want to focus on comes from 1 Corinthians 9:25, the *"Incorruptible crown."* This crown was known in Paul's day to be the victor's crown. I have yet to find one *"crown"* given to those who fight demons, but this one, in particular, is for those who have chosen to be faithful to the One who placed them here for Yahweh's purposes.

> ## The victor's crown belongs to those who have chosen to be faithful in the place of devotion.

Paul tells us that those who desire the victor's crown are *"temperate in all things."* In other words, there is a lot that this person lays down to lay hold of the prize. It's another call to a *"one thing"* focus. What is the prize? It's plain and simple, Jesus!

Next, we explore the breastplate of righteousness. This piece of armor is not the breastplate of a Roman soldier; it is *"of righteousness."* I love the revelation of righteousness because it eliminates all human involvement. This righteousness cannot be earned only inherited. It is the fact that *"He (Jesus) who knew no sin, became sin, that I through Him, might become the righteousness of God in Christ Jesus."* (2 Cor. 5:21, paraphrase)

This piece of armor is of vital importance because it is a constant reminder that the faithfulness of Jesus forever protects our new life in Christ and that God no longer sees us as *"sinner"* but as righteous as Jesus Himself. But, should we stop at the breastplate of righteousness or can we move on to a superior revelation called the *"robe of righteousness?"*

You are being called this day to great intimacy with Jesus. As a bride of Christ, He robes you for the bed-chamber. I want you to see the Holy Spirit as one taking the armor of war off of you, then replacing your dirt and blood-stained garments for the actual robe of Jesus Himself. Can you allow the Spirit to take you from a place of war to a bed-chamber of peace, free from the sounds of battle? Take rest in the comfort of His robe; this one piece has justified you forever to stay in constant communion with the Lover of your soul.

Then we celebrate the belt of truth. This one piece of the Lord is what holds the entire set of armor together. The incredible reality of righteousness will never fit you the way it was designed until you are tied tight by the belt of truth. The truth is because of the finished work of Jesus you are holy, justified, and beloved in the sight of God. This belt is essential no matter where you are in the depths of God because whether you are wearing the breastplate or the robe, truth keeps it all together.

Now that you have the crown of salvation, the robe of righteousness, and the belt of truth you can walk with the assurance of your shield of faith. Do I have to repeat it? This is not the Roman soldier's shield; this is the faith of God.

The faith of God should cause us to approach impossibility seated in the reality of invincibility.

With the faith of God, I can be assured, No weapon formed against me shall be able to prosper, a thousand may fall by my side and ten thousand at my right hand, but it shall not come nigh my dwelling. For the battle is not mine, it is the Lord's. What kind of shield do you need when you are confident in the one who has provided this armor? I do not see this as a big shield; I see myself divinely protected by Yahweh!

When you see yourself protected by God, you will then inherit the shoes of peace. These shoes were special ordered for you from the King who has a government of peace that will have no end. I know we have been taught that these shoes give us peace during the fight, but what if we could see it from the place of victory?

If you are seated in the heavenly realm, in the One, who was told to *"sit down until I make all your enemies a footstool for your feet,"* would you put dirty boots on His footstool. These shoes look a lot like slippers to me. The Apostle Paul said to those in Rome, *"The God of peace will soon crush Satan under your feet."* (Romans 16:20) With a warfare conscience, we see ourselves stomping the enemy, but actually, there is no need for boots when the God of peace will crush Satan under the feet which are propped up with Jesus on the footstool.

Finally, because we are seated in the slippers of peace, you can now correctly wield the sword of the Spirit which are the living promises of God. You no longer swing the sword out of fear, but with precision. The writers of Hebrews called the word of God, *"alive and powerful...sharper than the sharpest two-edged sword, cutting between soul and spirit."* (Hebrews 4:12, NLT)

The sword is *OF* the Spirit.

> ## You swing the sword by direction of the Spirit and not from a reaction to the adversary.

Because we have not allowed the word of God to divide between soul and spirit in our hearts we use the word of God for soulish purposes. We war for what we see in the natural and cannot see the victory already made possible by speaking the word of God alone.

According to Revelation 19:15 Christ is seated on a white horse and a sharp sword proceeds from His mouth. So if we are genuinely in Christ, then the sword is not even wielded by hand, but it proceeds from our mouth. This is when you know you have found a weapons upgrade. Remember my reference to the *"infantry?"* These are the *"foot soldiers"* who have less experience, but once these men gained experience, they were called up to the *"Calvary."*

When you are called up to the *"Calvary,"* you remain seated with the assistance of a horse carrying you into battle. From an elevated place of being seated, you can more effectively battle. So do you want to continue in the way you were taught or His way, by revelation? If you are in hand-to-hand, it is because you are still battling in the soulish realm. The seated posture of the Calvary is reserved for those walking in the Spirit.

Now you may be thinking I've gone too far this time. I never disregarded the foundation of Ephesians 6; I just said that's not a good place to stop. Does a crown, robe, and slippers seem too far-fetched for you? Beloved identity sees this way different than the cowards of Saul on the hillside being taunted by a giant. Only the government of Saul believes in putting warfare garments on. David, whose name means *"beloved,"* knew there was no need for armor because of his previous history of victory with Yahweh!

Would you be willing to let
go of an inferior garment to
believe that "beloved
identity" and intimacy is
enough to face giants?

Could you see yourself crowned and robed instead of in the infantry? This armor you have been given is of God because of all that Jesus has done. If you will put on salvation, righteousness, truth, peace, faith, and wield the sword of the Spirit, you will enjoy victory every time.

CHAPTER 10

COME UP HERE

If you have made it this far with me on the journey, you are probably still wondering, if victory belongs to the Lord then what is my place? This book was not intended to answer all the questions of spiritual warfare, nor to explain all the mysteries of the Spirit-realm. This whole journey has been to set your heart on a pilgrimage of face-to-face communion with Jesus free from the fear and overemphasis of the demonic realm.

I wrote this manuscript as provocation for an invitation into a lifestyle of devotion, not a long drawn out theological discourse. With that said, I believe John the Beloved, gives us the call that I want you to see when he recorded his encounter in Revelation 4:1.

"After these things I looked, and behold, a door standing open in heaven. And the first voice which I heard was like a trumpet speaking

with me, saying, 'Come up here, and I will show you things which must take place after this." (Rev. 4:1, NKJV)

Placed on an island to be abandoned by society, John was caught up in the Spirit on the Lord's day. This one invitation to *"come up here"* has changed my lens of warfare forever. This door is a point of access to the heavenly place you are called to live from. The voice that draws you is like the trumpet blast that calls men into victory formation. You are destined to dwell, sit, and decree from the throne room of God.

We know that Jesus is seated at the right hand of the Father and from His throne proceeds thunders, lightning, rainbows, and voices. Take a moment to recognize that tucked away in the lap of Christ is your seat. The four living creatures are swirling around you. You can hear the sound of the elder's crowns being cast onto the sea of glass. The cries of *"holy, holy, holy"* are almost deafening. Your seat is rumbling with thunder and flashes of light peal out from that seat constantly. This is a seat of authority, but you will know it as your seat of peace.

When you take your place *"in Him"* you will soon learn what Paul meant when he penned the words of Romans 16:20, *"...and the God of peace will soon crush Satan under your feet."* (Rom. 16:20, NKJV)

What is there to fear when all of your enemies are under your feet?

This has been made available to you by the blood of the spotless Lamb, Yeshua, the Christ, the Son of the living God! This is far above the war in the cosmos with no demon in sight. Once you have found this place of *"awe"* warfare does not seem a worthy thought or cause.

Jesus sits in this seat of eternity. So when it comes to casting out demons, He described it like flicking a bug off of your arm with the finger of God. It's just an ant. Many that magnify or overemphasize spiritual warfare are motivated ultimately by fear. Their problem is not a lack of authority; Christ has freely given it. The problem is perspective. They describe demons like the ten spies giving the evil report back to Moses concerning the promise land. But friend, when you sit in this seat of peace, you will never again see yourself as a grasshopper, hopeless, and helpless. This is the seat where all battles were won for all of eternity.

During the summer of 2015, we were invited to be apart of a tent meeting in northern Ohio. The Lord had been speaking to me all week about eagles. I did not have any insight into what the Lord was saying, but I knew the word *"eagles"* kept coming up in my spirit. As we got to the tent that day, I was telling the host pastor what I had been hearing. That's when one of his friends spoke up and said, *"While we were setting up the tent, two eagles came screaming over the top of the tent."* I knew the Lord was saying something because now I had two witnesses.

When you find yourself getting swirled in the prophetic, there is only one remaining thing to do…Google what you hear. I began researching why eagles scream. There were several reasons, but the one that caught my attention was to call eagles that are grounded to come up and take flight. This is a call that I believe is coming from the Spirit of the Lord. We have allowed fear, negativity, and doubt to so weary us that we have become grounded.

The church of America has looked more like chickens than eagles. We have been grounded by the culture of fear that permeates our atmosphere. Instead of flying high we settled for walking on land. But I hear the cry of Isaiah the prophet saying, *"But those who wait upon the Lord shall renew their strength; They shall mount up with wings like eagles, they shall run and not be weary, They shall walk and not faint."* (Isa. 40:31, NKJV)

The call of devotion is where we learn to mount up with wings like eagles. It was this place of devotion that John the Revelator took flight and wrote the entire book of Revelation. What mysteries, revelation, wisdom, understanding, cures for diseases, and solutions for international problems have yet to be discovered because we remain grounded? The Lord is calling for His eagles to come up here so He can show them things to come.

The second day at the tent meeting, the song of the Lord came by way of *"Somewhere Over The Rainbow."* It was a time of deep intimacy and joy in the Presence of the Lord. That's when the second call of the eagle came to me. The Lord said,

 "Eagles don't fight with serpents, they take them up,"

So right there in the middle of service, I went to a second great Biblical resource, *"Youtube."* I typed in exactly what I heard. This is where it got more interesting.

The first video that appeared was from National Geographics. A bald eagle is soaring high above the land. During the flight, the eagle spots a serpent in the water. The eagle begins his descent from thousands of feet away. The eagle can detect prey at fifty-miles out. As the eagle approaches the water, with his wings extended, one talon grabs the head of the serpent, while the other claw wraps around the body.

The eagle takes flight with the snake effortlessly. There is no fight, only the wiggling body of the serpent, and suddenly it dangles as they have reached an altitude where the serpent can no longer live. There is a place where serpents cannot live, *"above the snake line."* This is where Jesus wants us to live, at an altitude where the serpent can't live, a place where you don't have to fight on the ground, but you take the serpent up!

Could you dare to believe with me that you can learn to fly? Can you see it, instead of men struggling through addiction programs we could teach them to live in an altitude where serpents are no longer a threat? The writer of Hebrews tells of this place when he wrote that we could come *"boldly before the throne of grace…"* (Hebrews 4:16, NKJV) Why would you spend your life in such an altitude where you have to fight hand-to-hand on the ground? Yet, many believers find themselves dealing with serpents hand-to-hand when you could participate in an air strike.

It's time to move on as the writer of Hebrews declares, *"…leaving the discussion of the elementary principles of Christ, let us go on to perfection,"* (Hebrews 6:1, NKJV). Many believers are looking for serpents under every rock and behind every bush. Jesus never intended for us to live in reaction to our adversary. So when we spot a snake in the water, an air strike is all that is necessary.

In early 2016, the Lord said to tell his weary ones among the prayer movement that it's time for a weapons upgrade. The Lord is moving us from a sword to a seat. It's what my Apostle, Damon Thompson calls *"out of hand-to-hand combat into releasing airstrikes."* I want to get this word deep into the heart of weary intercessors that have labored for years with the heavy hand of the sword. It's time for promotion from proximity. You have a seat of peace *"in Him."* This is your place of authority.

It's time to quit swinging with fear in the dark. Take your place as kings and priests unto God, release decrees, and learn to rest in the finished work of Christ. It would be an insult to a soldier if he were faithfully serving in the military and did not get a promotion in rank. It would be abnormal for a child not to become a man. So why is it crazy to think we could not mature in the area of warfare?

Before you get nervous, I'm not throwing out the sword of the Spirit. Many think that when you share something new, it automatically means you throw out the foundation.

We are not dismantling the
Biblical foundation of
spiritual warfare; we are just
building upon it with
fresh revelation.

According to Revelation 19:15, the one seated on a white horse has a sharp sword which proceeds out of His mouth that conquers nations!

When you look at Moses and Joshua, both the sword and a seat were necessary. However, without Moses seated upon the rock and his hands lifted the battle would continue to wage. I believe this is a picture of how intimacy with Jesus produces dominion. We are nothing more than the sons of Sceva trying to perform exorcisms without being seated on the rock of devotion.

You may impress others with how well you handle your sword. But if you aren't intimate with Jesus, the enemy knows you have no actual authority. You have head knowledge and facts. Those who are seated on the rock of fellowship have a revelation that the victory has been accomplished! It's time we quit pushing things back by the proficiency of our sword and start winning by staying seated in the place of victory!

CHAPTER 11

ANGELIC ASSISTANCE

A ny time we dive into the subject of angels people get very nervous. Let's face facts; people have developed doctrines on the angelic that are bizarre, even leading some into deception. However, I think it is a piece that can give us greater confidence in devotion without being distracted by focusing on the demonic.

In the days of Israel's captivity in Babylon, there was significant angelic activity occurring in the land. In Daniel 4, Nebuchadnezzar has a dream of a large tree in the middle of the earth. The tree grew tall and strong, reaching into the heavens for the whole world to see. It was beautiful, green, and full of fruit. But in an instant, an angel coming down from heaven shouted, *"Cut down the tree and lop off its branches!"*

This dream was a word of judgment given to the King of Babylon because of his pride, wicked past, and his lack of mercy to the poor. The interesting part of this story is that Yahweh shows the king and Daniel that two things are happening that will cause him to fall, and they are recorded in Daniel 4:17, *"This decision is by the decree of the watchers, And the sentence by the word of the holy ones,"*

The watchers are *"`iyr"* (Aramaic), meaning angels and the holy ones are *"qaddiysh"* (Aramaic), meaning saints. So judgment on the most powerful man of the world was going to be unleashed if there was no personal repentance by the king. These *"watchers"* are investigative angels who are sent to respond to the cry of the saints. If they discover that what these holy ones are saying is true, then they execute the judgment of God to make things right. You will find Nebuchadnezzar did not repent and for seven years roamed his land like a wild animal.

Nowhere in the text does it say that the holy ones were aware of any manifestations of demonic activity. They were crying out for the mercy of God and for justice to be served. The holy ones had one responsibility, devotion. There was no need for a plan; they did not have to identify the principality over the region or take the high place. Hearts set on Yahweh in the area of prayer was all that was necessary.

Daniel was a man of great prophetic wisdom, from interpreting dreams to having visions, we see him as one of God's chosen in Israel's darkest days. Daniel was a man of prayer, and it is from his encounters that many have developed a theology about Spiritual

Warfare. But I think many, out of infatuation with how the Spirit realm works, missed the whole cause for the angelic interaction.

As a good steward of the prophetic, Daniel knew the prophecies of Jeremiah concerning Israel's captivity would last only seventy years. In his own words, Daniel said, *"I set my face toward the Lord."* (Dan. 9:3) One man decided to experience face-to-face communion with God. He fasted, prayed, and made a personal confession. He repented for the sins of his nation and reminded Yahweh the promises He spoke through the Prophet Jeremiah.

We all know the story of Daniel's desperation, many of us have even participated in what is now called the *"Daniel Fast."* But after twenty-one days of Daniel's appeal to God, he received an angelic visitor. The messenger said, *"Do not fear, Daniel, for from the first day that you set your heart to understand, and to humble yourself before your God, your words were heard; and I have come because of your words. ¹³But the prince of the kingdom of Persia withstood me twenty-one days; and behold, Michael, one of the chief princes, came to help me, for I had been left alone there with the kings of Persia. ¹⁴Now I have come to make you understand what will happen to your people in the latter days, for the vision refers to many days yet to come."* (Daniel 10:12-14, NKJV)

This is where we first learn in the Canon of scripture about prince spirits and the battle of the cosmos, a war between angels and demons. But here is the part we miss. Daniel was unaware of the warfare. His concern was the humility of his own heart and to come before God with the promises of His word. He did not identify the prince spirit over Persia to receive this breakthrough.

The angel was not informing Daniel how to war in the heaven-lies, only to explain the reason for the delay, and to assure Daniel that when an answer is needed Michael would find a way to break through! As surprising as this information is, we can't build an entire theology of Spiritual Warfare from this Old Testament passage; Especially, since Jesus declared to a man the eternal truth of His open heaven in John 1:51 where messengers ascend and descend without the hindrance of the demonic.

Don't lose sight of Daniel's encounter with the angelic. This will change the way we see Spiritual Warfare, and it will draw us into the greatest depths of personal intimacy with Jesus. The angel said the first thing I must remind you of is how much Yahweh loves you. How we settled for the inferior understanding of angels and demons fighting before the finished work of Christ is baffling to me. However, we missed the essential aspect of devotion in the face of great adversity: We are dearly loved!

The God of all things seen and unseen adores me, and to protect our intimacy, He sends angels to war so we can enjoy face-to-face without distraction. I know this is hard for some to hear because you thought that battling the demonic required your best spiritual effort.

> But if Daniel didn't have to
> acknowledge the demonic
> for a breakthrough in the
> Old Testament, I'm sure not
> going to do it while I'm
> covered in the BLOOD
> of Jesus.

It's time to make a shift; we are the bride, not boots on the ground. Angels are the only army required within the Kingdom. These angels with swords drawn guard access to Eden protecting our intimacy to make sure we don't get distracted from face-to-face. It's time to meet the captain of the host of the Lord who revealed himself to Joshua. (Joshua 5:13-14) In Hebrew, the word hosts is translated *"tsebaah,"* which means soldiers organized and equipped for war. Jesus is the host of angelic soldiers equipped for battle.

This angelic host is created to carry out the plans of Yahweh. Psalm 103:20 says, *"Praise the Lord, you angels, you mighty ones who carry out His plans, listening for each of His commands."* In Tim Sheet's book, *"Angel Armies"* he writes that this angel army does what Kingdom armies do:

- Guard and protect a king and his kingdom
- Guard the inhabitants of the kingdom
- Implement the king's strategies, plans, and laws
- Protect and patrol borders
- Enforce the king's jurisdiction

- Stewards the king's resources
- Facilitates and enforces covenants (King's decrees)
- Keeps weapons and weapon systems in operation condition
- War against threats to the kingdom
- Protect and assist a king's family (heirs)

If this is true and we see angelic assistant through the perspective of devotion and the Kingdom why are we so focused on the demonic? Are we not heirs of Christ and are they not ministering spirits? We are not just inhabitants of this Kingdom; we are the bride of the King! So step inside the Garden and enjoy the Bridegroom, the angel with flaming sword drawn still protects its borders.

CHAPTER 12

BRIDAL
IDENTIFICATION

I n the fall of 2016, our Kingdom family would be forever changed by one small portion of the Bible, the Song of Solomon. For three months we stared at eight chapters of a song most neglected by the church and at best treated as Christian erotica. How could such a glorious picture of Christ's love for His bride remain hidden from the American Christian?

There I sat around my firepit, sometimes from 8 am until midnight, being transformed by the gaze of my Bridegroom King! As I meditated on this reality, I wondered how a thirty-two-year-old and in church my whole life could count on one hand the messages I heard about being the bride of Christ.

Besides smelling like a campfire for 90 days, I had forever lost the argument about why He should not love me, and it has brought me into my most tender days of devotion.

For years I had struggled in the condemnation of Pentecostal theology, never hearing one voice tell me that with one look I ravished the heart of Jesus. No one introduced me to the idea that I was one betrothed to Christ. Instead, I felt like God tried to tolerate my frequent failures. Many days I sat in my little plastic Adirondack chair pondering how such a truth be kept such a secret in my lifetime.

The scales that blinded our eyes from this truth was our ministry ambitions. We found more value in our works than in our identity. I learned to preach way before I knew who I was in Christ, let alone knowing myself as dearly loved!

> ## Although my zeal for the ministry caused me to experience a measure of success, it did not take long for it to destroy my vineyard within.

I became a victim of performance Christianity, always caring for my brother's ministry vineyards, wondering like a prostitute, losing sight of the one I loved. My salvation was fragile, so if I didn't pray enough my anointing was questionable, and God forbid my message didn't crescendo into full altars with bodies on the floor.

Ministry outside of proper identity became my warfare. What could I have avoided if I had fathers in my life more concerned with my life of devotion instead of what I was going to preach? We need fathers like the Apostle Paul who are committed to presenting a generation as a virgin bride to Christ. Fathers who will challenge false teaching and make sure the children of God are not getting wrong information. Paul was so concerned for the church in Corinth that he spent four chapters (2 Corinthians 10-14) about the issue of false teachers and central to that text was the words *"war"* and *"warfare."*

Paul saw the people he loved coming into bondage. These so-called *"apostles"* were hindering the people's ability to walk in love and to remain committed to Christ in pure devotion. Paul was warning them of not heeding to another Jesus or a different gospel than what they first experienced. These thoughts were building up strongholds that were in agreement with Satan.

Paul was encouraging those in Corinth to cast down these high things that were exalting themselves against the knowledge of God and come back to the simplicity of devotion to Christ. How does Paul start demolishing this teaching? By talking to the church about bridal identification. *"I am jealous for you with godly jealousy. For I have betrothed you to one husband, that I may present you as a chaste virgin to Christ."* (2 Cor. 11:2)

You are betrothed, legally engaged to the Lord. This is not engagement as we have seen it modeled in our society. During those days, engagement meant legally married. A legal ceremony took place before witnesses. It was binding; for at least a year they did not live together but would prepare their hearts as the man would prepare a place for them to dwell together.

If you have been born-again, then you are legally married to Christ. You are desired, chosen, and beautiful. Song of Solomon 1:9 says, *"My dearest one, let me tell you how I see you-you are so thrilling to me."* So the essence of your whole process is not to prepare you for winning a war but preparing for the day of consummation. Mike Bickle said, *"This information will stand against the arguments in your mind that you're worthless, you're nothing, you're forgotten, you're neglected, you're unimportant."*

We need a fresh revelation of our bridal identity. It roots our heart in the love of God. It shows us our place in Christ far above the works of darkness and reveals a greater appreciation for the angelic host! Knowing the protection of our heavenly Father and ravished heart of our Bridegroom King should be enough to keep our minds away from inferior thoughts and pursuits.

There is no greater picture of this position in Christ than what we find in Song of Solomon 6:12 when the Shulamite bride said, *"Then suddenly my longings transported me next to my beloved prince, sitting with Him in his royal chariot. We were lifted up together."* This a picture of desire and passion in devotion that places us in proximity to our Beloved, safe within the super-weapon of the ancient world, His royal chariot.

As I stood to preach in Crestview, FL in September of 2016 I heard the Lord say to me, *"A new reformation is coming, more significant than Luther's day. The message of bridal identification will be significant to the remnant, and we should expect persecu-*

tion as Luther did for justification by faith alone." I recognize that not everyone will understand this shift in identity, but we must learn how to stay in the royal chariot of His love without defending ourselves.

Five hundred years ago a young man, Martin Luther, nailed the *"95 theses"* on the door of a church hoping to start a conversation but instead caused a reformation. He was sick of the systems of men and the religion that kept people from knowing Jesus intimately. And once again, we find ourselves in the infancy stages of a new reformation.

> # Reformers are coming forth from intimate devotion to Jesus as lovestruck brides who will not let popular church culture sway her.

She honors the past but refuses to live in it. She dreams of the future, but her focus is on being present in the Presence of her Bridegroom now.

Her enemy will not be the world, because she will cause them to wonder. Her enemy will be the religious trying to silence her passion, for it reveals their pursuit of guarding theological positions, unbiblical ambitions, and finances. Her devotion to Jesus will expose that they have nothing to offer now, only promises of a future to come and stories of generation's past.

This is not her time of battle, but her time in the bedchamber. She is leaving the house of warfare filled with demonic fascination and has moved into the house of wine filled with Spirit intoxication. Yes, the battle rages, but she is not aware for her Bridegroom is the host of heaven's armies that are sent to war on her behalf. Bride and Groom speak back and forth, while angelic intervention guards their intimacy.

Will you answer this call of devotion as a bride to Bridegroom?

> # Are you willing to be misunderstood by the warriors on the battlefield to cultivate intimacy as a bride?

Or do you have to be understood to protect your reputation? I would rather stand before Him on the day of Judgment, and He knows my name than have all the accolades of ministry and Him say *"Depart from me you worker of lawlessness, I never knew you intimately."*

CHAPTER 13

THE END OF SATAN'S KINGDOM

How controversial would it be for me to announce the end of Satan's Kingdom? Would it make you nervous if I told you to live in such a way that you don't war, instead you gather spoils? I would be considered a *"no-more-war"* heretic who is leading the body of Christ astray. I suppose that would be good company since the Pope said Martin Luther was a *"wild boar"* that invaded the vineyard of the Lord.

Nevertheless, two thousand years ago, Jesus announced the end of Satan's Kingdom before He ever embraced the cross of His crucifixion. In Matthew 12:25-30, a crowd had gathered to see what Jesus would do with a blind, mute, demon-possessed man.

With no act of exorcism recorded within the text, Matthew said, *"Jesus healed him instantly."*

As the crowd was in total bewilderment, one group, the Pharisees had to chime in. *"He casts out demons by the power of Satan, the prince of demons."* Jesus supernaturally perceiving their thoughts, confronted them by telling this parable:

"Any kingdom that fights against itself will end up in ruins. And any family or community splintered by strife will fall apart. ²⁶So if Satan casts out Satan, he is making war on himself. How then could his kingdom survive? ²⁷So if Satan empowers me to cast out demons, who empowers your exorcists to cast them out? Go ask them, for what they do proves you're wrong in your accusations. ²⁸On the other hand, if I drive out demons by the power of the Spirit of God, then the end of Satan's kingdom has come! ²⁹Who would dare enter the house of a mighty man and steal his property? First, he must be overpowered and tied up by one who is stronger than he. Then his entire house can be plundered and every possession stolen. ³⁰So join with me, for if you're not on my side you are against me. And if you refuse to help me gather the spoils, you are making things worse." (Matthew 12:25-30)

The Pharisees believe in casting out demons. We know that because they had exorcists casting out demons as well. What the Pharisees did not believe was in the One who had instantly healed this man. The real issue of this text isn't over Jesus' authority; it's about His identity. These men wanted Jesus killed because He claimed to be the Son of God. They were frustrated because Jesus had performed a miracle by the power of the Spirit and not from the rituals of religion.

They could not comprehend how Jesus could have the audacity to do these works from the identity as a Son of God. According to writings from Origen, Josephus, and an article written by Rabbi Geoffrey Dennis[3], the religious had made Spiritual Warfare liturgical, a public event either performed in the synagogue or in the presence of ten men. The process began with ritual purification anointing himself with water and oil.

Rabbi Geoffrey continues describing deliverance in those days having to *"include interviewing the demon, taking personal history, in order to understand what is motivating the spirit and so better effect the removal."* In another quote, he said, *"The goal of the interview is to eventually learn the name of the evil spirit. The exorcist then uses the power of the demonic spirit's name to 'overpower' it, by round after round of scripted ritual actions involving threats and rebukes, getting more intense and invasive with each effort."*

I want to take you into the words of Jesus spoken back to this outlandish accusation from the Pharisees about casting out demons by the power of demons. His response is a direct aim at their behavior. Were the Pharisees not fighting against their own Kingdom? Were they not a splintered family and community? The answer is yes, they had separated themselves not by the law of God but by their own rules and rituals.

Jesus continues His response to the Pharisees by asking, *"Who empowers your exorcists to cast them out?"* This is an interesting question now considering Rabbi Geoffrey's article because they were casting out demons by the power of demons; using the power of the demonic spirit's name to cast it out. I don't believe Jesus was trying to say that what He was doing was the same as the Jewish exorcists; I think He was trying to point out that they were doing what they had just accused Jesus of.

In light of this passage and the historical view of Jewish exorcism, I want to ask this question: Have we allowed the leaven of the Pharisees to influence our understanding of Spiritual Warfare? Do we depend on our works and mythical rituals? We have to ask the question because these practices have crept into the practice of *"deliverance ministries"* in our day. This is not speculation, in fact, I discovered over the years several churches where I had ministered at, had teams of people who would take someone manifesting an evil spirit out of the sanctuary into a private room where the demon was recorded, interviewed, and then exorcised.

We must ask this question because of how much energy and time ministries are spending teaching this generation about demonic spirits, to the point where Jezebel, Leviathan, and Absolom get a spotlight while the Holy Spirit is only used to glorify their altar calls. Entire classes of demonology are taught in Bible schools across the nation. Books are written because of an infatuation with evil spirits. I think it's the best we could do in light of our results.

This needs to be confronted in our day. We have allowed the leaven of the Pharisees to creep into our way of thinking as it pertains to Spiritual Warfare to the point where certain ministries fight against those who refuse their methods and believe identity as a son and the power of the Holy Spirit is enough. We don't need to interview the demonic, discover rituals and practices; we must receive the revelation of who we are in Christ and understand our dependence on the Holy Spirit's power alone!

Jesus said, *"If I drive out demons by the power of the Spirit of God, then the end of Satan's Kingdom has come!"* (Matt. 12:28, TPT) I'm not sure that is a statement many are ready to receive; however, it is what Jesus said. He was declaring to the people that He had bound the strongman of house (Satan), and it was time for them to join Him in gathering the spoils of victory. This does not sound like the fear-based rhetoric we hear coming from the pulpits of America.

Recently, a prayer leader announced that since we have dealt with a particular spirit in our nation now one much stronger was coming. This announcement so grieved me. It seems that in the Spiritual Warfare camp we brace ourselves for Matthew 12:43-45 without acknowledging the foundational statement of Matthew 12:28. To put it plainly we have a religious lens as it pertains to the demonic so instead of embracing that it is the end of Satan's kingdom we brace for the possibility of spirits coming back seven times stronger. Where does this thinking come from?

When Jesus describes the activity of the demonic in Matthew 12:43-45, He says, *"When a demon is cast out of a person, it roams around a dry region, looking for a place to rest, but never finds it. 44 Then it says, 'I'll return to the house I moved out of,' and so it goes back, only to find that the house is vacant, warm, and ready for it to move back in. 45 So it goes looking for seven other demons more evil than itself, and they all enter together to live there. Then the person's condition becomes much worse than it was in the beginning. This describes what will also happen to the people of this evil generation."*

We must remember that Jesus is still speaking to the same group of Pharisees that have accused Him of demonic activity. The verse above is where we get the understanding of how the demonic works. But the emphasis should not be upon the demonic, but rather the condition of the home. I believe this a picture of what Jesus said religion was doing to their generation. They could displace spirits, clean up the house, and even set it straight. But they were missing the main ingredient. The power of the Spirit residing in the home.

Jesus is saying to us when we discover our identity and allow the power of His Spirit to reside within us we need not worry about evil spirits finding a home vacant, warm, and ready to move back in. We are no longer surviving from the regular application of religious principles. We have become new creatures, our identity is in Christ, and the Holy Spirit that drives evil spirits out now can move in! It is in this place of identity that we can join with Jesus in gathering the spoils, and could we dare to join Jesus in His announcement that the end of Satan's Kingdom has come?

CONCLUSION

Some of my favorite books are those who are willing to give up their secret sauce in one chapter we call the *"Conclusion."* A conclusion is defined in two ways, (1) the end or finish of an event or process, (2) a judgment or decision reached by reasoning. I have finished this book; however, I'm still in process. Maybe I should even consider calling this Volume One, why because I'm on a journey and my theology is evolving.

We must stand with Jesus and Luther and say *"Devil, you lie!"* That one little word should cause us to question anything we have been taught about by a calloused heart religion. Satan is not an omnipresent or omnipotent dragon. He's still the same crafty serpent who deceived Eve in the Garden.

> We cannot be silent and allow our generation to continue the cycle of fear and fascination with the inferior world of darkness.

Principalities have been disarmed, and Jesus holds the keys to death, hell, and the grave! Yahweh sits on His throne and laughs over the plans of His enemies and then bids us ask Him for the nations. We are His conquerors!

We cannot use our Light to place a spotlight on the Kingdom of darkness nor should we call our generation to the battlefield. To not rest in the finished work is to insult the blood of Jesus and it is to say we are more efficient in the cosmos than Michael. We can't do it.

We cannot use spiritual warfare as another excuse to avoid the life of devotion. If the enemy has authority our lives, it is because somewhere in the conversation we agreed with him. So let us say yes to the garden-life, walking with God in the cool-of-the-day, enjoying face-to-face. If the enemy has something to say, my response will be...*"It is written."*

I see a company that will become like children willing to embrace mystery. They will be teachable and set their hearts to be delivered from the narcissism of being know-it-alls. We understand that the weapon which is mighty in God for the pulling down of strongholds is the knowledge of God, and that experiential knowledge is the pathway to victory.

We will be faithful to the call of devotion to Jesus. To remain single-minded to please the One who called, abstaining from fleshly lusts that war against the soul, and bringing every thought captive to the obedience of Christ. With each step of obedience, we expand Eden's borders causing darkness to lose more territory.

> This is the hour of great dominion for the church, and it will not come from the proficiency of our sword, rather from our unwavering commitment to one thing: the Great Commandment.

We are not ignorant of Satan's devices, yet we refuse to become experts because we have a superior fascination: the knowledge of God!

We understand that victory belongs to Yahweh. He is our warrior who fights our enemies and allows us to gather the spoils. We must learn to stand still and see the salvation of the Lord. The Light is invading the darkness, yokes are being destroyed, and burdens removed from necks, so remove your boots and uniforms as fuel for the fires of devotion and prepare yourself with bridal adornments in the bedchamber of intimacy.

We will not make theology adapt to the multiplicity of our circumstances; we will stand in the victory that triumphs over the world, our faith. May you see this as your invitation to develop a robust theology of victory! When you do, we will begin to see more clearly that the kingdoms of this world will become the kingdoms of our God and His Christ as a reality in our day.

May you look back to this book as a flashpoint that propelled you into a journey with Yahweh! You may have read something that rubbed you wrong, search it out. You may have found something in the manuscript that left you with questions, ask Yahweh to show you. I wrote this to send you into walks with Yahweh in the garden of His pleasure not make you co-dependent on my answers.

Who knows, maybe one day we will cross paths and have time to talk. It's my prayer that when we do, it will be stories of great victory, faith, and encounters and never again conversations that speak of constant attacks and warfare on every side. Instead, you will say, He invaded my world with His goodness, and I was never the same.

This book may be over, but your story of victory has just begun. God bless you and may this book be a continual wind to your walks with Yahweh in the cool of the day! I can't wait to hear your experiences, questions, and testimonies from this book. Feel free to contact me at: **mark@frontporchpod.com**

REFERENCES

[1]   https://www.challies.com/articles/hymn-stories-a-mighty-fortress-is-our-god/

[2]   https://www.anxietycentre.com/anxiety-statistics-information.shtml

[3]   https://www.myjewishlearning.com/article/jewish-exorcism/

Printed in Great Britain
by Amazon